HAROLD KLEMP

LOVE—
THE
KEYSTONE
OF LIFE

HAROLD KLEMP

ECKANKAR

Minneapolis

ABOUT THIS BOOK: *Love—The Keystone of Life* is compiled from Harold Klemp's writings. These selections originally appeared in his books published by Eckankar.

Printed in U.S.A.

Compiled by John Kulick
Edited by Joan Klemp, Anthony Moore,
and Mary Carroll Moore
Cover photo by Jim Brandenburg/Minden Pictures
Text photo by Robert Huntley
Cover design by Doug Munson

Publisher's Cataloging-in-Publication
(Provided by Quality Books, Inc.)

Klemp, Harold.
Love--the keystone of life / Harold Klemp.
p. cm.
LCCN 2004102752
ISBN 1-57043-208-2

1. Eckankar (Organization)--Doctrines 2. Spiritual life--Eckankar (Organization) 3. Love   I. Title.

BP605.E3S65 2004   299'.93
                                        QBI04-700089

∞ The paper used in this publication meets the minimum requirements of the American National Standard for Information Sciences—Permanence of Paper for Printed Library Materials, ANSI Z39.48-1984.

Contents

DEAR READER

Love—The Keystone of Life is the second volume in Harold Klemp's compelling "Immortality of Soul Series" of gift books.

The purpose of this book is to help us remember that love is the keystone of our lives. Our true identity is Soul, a spark of God. To keep in touch with our true nature as Soul, we must give love wherever and whenever we can. This is the divine law.

In these pages you will discover truths that are keys to a life of greater love, wisdom, and freedom. There is so much God has to give you and me. But the rules and codes we live by sometimes restrict us—without letting us know there is a higher, divine law, the Law of Love.

So what is the reason for living? Life is God's blessing to each Soul (you). We are here to learn to give and receive love. That's what's going on behind the scenes in this great laboratory of life.

Take one quote each day, and contemplate its meaning. Love, the keystone of life, is at your fingertips. May you gradually come to experience the greatest love of all.

GIVING—THE SECRET TO GETTING

*T*here is a respect that we must give to each other as Soul, recognizing the uniqueness of the other as a spark of God.

*I*f you are willing to give another person his state of consciousness, you have at least the right to expect the same for yourself.

*T*o let others have their freedom reflects the harmony and goodwill that is within.

What we're trying to do is open our hearts to divine love, so we can become instruments of God, so we can start serving God.

*I*f you are not able to love your loved ones, how can you love God?

Approach life with common sense, and sometimes just with common courtesy.

*O*nce we gain reassurance of ourselves as Soul, we gain confidence in life.

*T*he opportunity for growth is there, where we learn how to give.

*F*acing life gracefully is probably the first step to giving of yourself to others.

They aren't separate qualities. The quality of being graceful in your dealings with other people or in giving of yourself to life go together. They complement each other.

*W*hen we come into this world and take on responsibilities, this is where we find our spiritual unfoldment.

*I*f you want something of great value, you're going to have to work hard for it. There's no free lunch; there is no easy street.

When you learn the lessons, when you understand the Law of Cause and Effect, you graduate to the realization of divine love. Your life becomes richer in the blink of an eye, because you have moved from the consciousness of the masses to the spiritual consciousness of God, of divine love.

LOVE DRIVES SOUL ON

*I*f I want to go somewhere, I would like to have the freedom to go there. And if I want this freedom for myself, I must be willing to allow it for other people. They must have the same freedom.

*T*here is such a thing as self-responsibility. But no one person can draw that line of self-responsibility for another.

*D*ivine truth is not apparent. It is not obvious. It's like pearls before the swine. The pearls are there, but people cannot see them unless in their hearts and minds they are ready to receive the gifts of God.

*P*eople think that the Holy Spirit speaks to us in the human voice. This can occur, but it usually happens when a messenger of God—an angel, for example—is sent to a human being. Then people hear a voice. But the pure Voice of God is music, the Audible Sound Current, the Holy Spirit.

*S*o often we think God's gifts come simply because we ask. For instance, we're in the privacy of our home, and we pray, "God, give me wisdom."

But sometimes God requires that you go out into the world. In other words, you have to stand up, put one foot in front of the other, and go look for wisdom, divine love, understanding, or whatever you're seeking. You have to be willing to go outside of yourself.

You have to give up some of your preconceived ideas about what God is, what divine love is. It means having the attitude of a child.

When times are hard, some people complain. And as they complain about the hard times, they shut themselves off from the opportunities that lie within their troubles.

Other people have learned to be patient. They look for the lessons within their hardships or troubles.

*L*ove God, and let others love God in their own way too. Set the example of what it means to be a lover of God.

*W*hen trouble comes, realize that you ultimately have created that problem for yourself, according to the Law of Karma, the Law of Cause and Effect. You created this problem for yourself because of a lack of knowledge of the ways of divine law.

The way to get this knowledge is not through a holy book or scripture. Scriptures can be guidelines. They can give you a clue of what life is all about, what the spiritual laws are. But ultimately it gets down to testing these laws in your daily life.

In other words, you have to experience life in order to grow spiritually. There is no other way.

*W*e like to have people around us who bring out the best in us. Especially if we are looking for the highest in life, especially if we are looking for the love and the truth of God. It's the old thing of birds of a feather flocking together. If you're an eagle, you want to be around eagles.

*Y*our behavior tells everybody where you are spiritually.

*I*f you would have love, you must first give love. And if you give divine love to others, you shall have divine love for yourself.

THE SLOW BURNING LOVE OF GOD

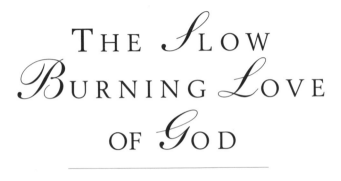

*T*he real reason for our being here is to open ourselves more to this burning love of God.

*I*t's a very humble love; it's a true love. Don't look too high, because you won't find it. The love of God is often very low where no one will look for it. And this is why so few people find it.

*T*his is the paradox of God's love. It's at once the most wonderful fulfillment in your spiritual life and at the same time it leaves you apart from others, in a way, because few people have ever had this burning love of God.

We have the greatest gift there is: the gift of life. And what we do from here on is up to us.

You have to be the master of your mind. And what part of you is the master of the mind? It has to be the heart.

*D*ivine love is something that is shared. In the same way it comes from God to people, it is shared from people to people, from people to pets, and from pets to people. It works very simply. Divine love doesn't have the barriers that the human mind makes.

The Light and Sound are the two aspects of God that speak to the human race, that speak to each Soul. The Light and Sound together are the Voice of God, what the Old and New Testaments call the Holy Spirit or Logos. Together, they are simply divine love.

*T*he Light of God may be yellow or blue or any of the other colors; It may look like a lamp, a spotlight, a flickering candle, or a lighthouse off in the distance. It may come as a soft glow, It may come as a piercing ray of light, or It may come as a bolt of lightning. It may come in any number of ways to your inner vision. But each time you see the Light of God, It will uplift you spiritually.

The counterpart to the Light of God is the Sound of God. The sounds of nature mimic this Sound of God—birds or musical instruments; the sound of a train, a plane, rockets, or crickets; or some other sound like the high energy of a motor or an engine. Again, this is the action of the Voice of God working within you to leave you a little better, a little bit more purified spiritually than you were before the experience.

*T*he Spiritual Exercises of ECK are simple contemplations; in a way they are equivalent to prayer.

Most people are used to prayers that ask something of God. They are used to telling God, "Do this for me. I want health. My finances aren't going very well; I need wealth."

In contemplation we shut our eyes, listen, and wait for God to speak to us. It's a whole different approach. Through the spiritual exercises and this contemplative effort, we learn to listen to the Voice of God. The Voice of God is the Holy Spirit, which we call the ECK.

The Golden-tongued Wisdom is a blending of inner truths with an outer experience of some kind, some everyday activity that you're doing.

If you want something to work, you've got to put your love into it.

✳

*Y*our ability to fill your heart with divine love depends on the strength of your desire for God.

THE PATH TO GOD

*T*he journey home to God is
what life is about. In a sense it's not even a
journey, it's an ongoing experience.

*P*eople are looking for adventure, and when we are not able to go inwardly and find this adventure, we look outwardly.

*I*t's that old catch-22: You've got to unfold slowly into the consciousness of wisdom to accept wisdom.

*S*ometimes the love is so strong, it's really incredible. It fills you with joy. It cleanses the heart, it purifies it, and it gives the person a readiness to accept more of God's love.

*A*s you receive more of the Sound and Light of ECK (the Holy Spirit), you get greater responsibility along with the greater freedom.

You need to be spiritually strong to handle experiences with the Light and Sound of God.

We do not become one with God. We maintain our distinctness, our individuality, as Co-workers with God.

*O*nce we set a goal, then all the things that happen in between are life's lessons.

*Y*ou can lose the fear of death. You are then able to enjoy this life and to live it fully.

We are as high on the path of spiritual consciousness as we've ever been.

You realize you can no longer form your spiritual path based on what someone else tells you.

*L*ook within for the answer whenever something comes up: What am I learning here? How can I get on top of this situation?

*W*hen you're ready, you're going
to find your next step on the spiritual path.

FROM DARKNESS TO LIGHT

*S*oul is light, a spark of God.

When the Light and Sound come into the inner vision, the Spiritual Eye, or the heart, you'll be filled with a joy and love you've never felt before.

*I*f you're in harmony with the spiritual principles at all, you're going to know that the life you have is the one you have created for yourself in some way, at some time. Today you are simply living out your own creation.

*S*pirit knows our problems and our situations, but It won't heal or cure them until we have come to an understanding of what they are.

*S*o many people tell God what to do. But if they would just listen to God sometimes, they would find it an enlightening experience.

Reincarnation is one of the basic principles of life. Another one is karma, cause and effect—that if you do something to another, whether good or bad, you're going to get the effect of it.

When we break a spiritual law, whether willfully or in ignorance, it sets up a series of events.

The five passions of the mind—greed, anger, lust, attachment, and vanity—this is what causes our karma.

*T*he singing of HU (pronounced like the word *hue*), this sacred prayer song which is the name of God, purifies the thoughts that lead to your actions.

To grow in Spirit, we must give up the old for the new.

As we raise ourselves in the spiritual consciousness, as we go higher, we are better able to solve the problems of life.

*W*e eventually come into full awareness of these divine laws, which operate whether we are aware of them or not.

When we are walking in Spirit, we have awareness and happiness. We have a life of action. This is the way of divine love.

*T*he Holy Spirit doesn't lead or live your life for you; It helps when you've made every effort for yourself.

When your heart is full of love,
what room is there for fear?

THE LESSONS OF LOVE AND THANKS

*T*here's no way to miss out on the blessings of God unless you turn your back on the love and thanks that are yours as a gift.

*I*f you give from your heart, this is the most valuable gift you can give any-one.

*W*hen we go through the experiences that are part of our everyday lives, often there are times of joy in between the lessons. But sometimes it seems there are a lot more rocks in our way than soft grass to walk on. There are always things underfoot, things to make us trip or stumble.

But these stumbling blocks can be stepping-stones. It depends on our attitude.

God is love, and Soul exists because God loves It.

*L*ife shall teach you better. If you don't get it now, you'll get it later.

*D*o you realize when you have the Sound and Light in your life, you are having actual communication with God?

*D*ivine Spirit works in Its own way, in Its own time.

*S*ometimes the Holy Spirit may work in a gentle way. It may give you just a nudge, a feeling of how to act, what to do.

*K*eep unfolding and opening yourself more as a clear vehicle for God, and as you do, your values will change.

*L*ook always to the inner, to the window of Soul.

*T*o get love, you must give love wherever and whenever you can, because that is the Law of Love.

RECOGNIZING GOD'S BLESSINGS

Recognizing God's blessings for us also means having to recognize God's blessings for other people.

*Y*ou are Soul. You are a light of God. And whatever your relationship with God is, that is your relationship with God, and it's your business. Not anyone else's.

*P*eople don't realize that God has provided all these different religions for a specific purpose: to fit all the different levels of consciousness that exist on earth.

How is a human being to judge
the spiritual state of another human being?

A better form of religion is letting other people love God in their own way.

*T*he point of any religion should be this: how to open your heart to love.

*P*eople who are in the top 5 percent of any religious group—if you're going to grade them by spirituality or closeness to God—have very much in common. They are generally people who are filled with love.

*I*f you can open your heart with love, you can tune in to God's will.

*L*ife will tell you what's right for you, and it will also tell you what's wrong for you. We call this the waking dream or the Golden-tongued Wisdom.

*T*his is one of the golden gifts of the people who are Co-workers with God: the ability to listen to others.

*G*od's blessings are always with you. You just need the eyes to see and the ears to hear.

BLESS THIS DAY

---

*E*verything happens for a purpose: to lift Soul higher and give It more experience.

*B*eing a Co-worker with God means continuing to develop—not just your creative powers, but your capacity to love.

*W*e are here on this earth with the opportunity to go home to God.

*W*e're talking about spiritual freedom. In the spiritual worlds, there are no slaves. You do not get ahead by crushing someone else underneath your foot. In the true spiritual worlds, it's a level playing field, and it's always a win-win situation.

You do not become one with God, even though you are Soul, a light of God. You become one with the Holy Spirit.

*N*ondirected prayer depends upon the divine power, the higher power. It depends upon the power of God. So whether you say "Thy will, not mine, be done," or as we in ECK say, "May the blessings be," this is the proper spiritual way to direct your own life.

If you have a health problem, or if you're having a problem finding work or keeping the job you have, or if you're having a problem with your loved one or someone not so loved—instead of saying, "God, help me be stronger," maybe just try "Thy will be done."

It's unconditional love that makes such a prayer. And this is important.

*I*f you have love and trust in the Holy Spirit, the ECK, then the love of God will flow to you just the way water flows from a faucet.

*B*less this day. And as we bless this day, we realize it was another opportunity to grow: to see, to know, to be.

These are aspects of Soul: to see, to know, to be. No matter what your age—whether you're a child, whether you're very old and have seen all the seasons of life many, many times—as long as you have the love of God in your heart, you will always have this instinctive urge to see another day, and to say good night to this day as Bless this day.

HU—THE MOST BEAUTIFUL PRAYER

A nondirected prayer means that we're willing to let the Holy Spirit take care of the affairs in our life according to the divine plan instead of our personal plan.

HU, this ancient name for God, is a love song to God. You can sing it. And in singing it or holding it in your mind during times of need, it becomes a prayer. It becomes a prayer of the highest sort.

The Holy Spirit works on a personal level with every person.

*I*f you're in trouble, in pain, in need of comfort, or in need of love, sing HU quietly to yourself.

If you know how to sing HU, you can open yourself to the Holy Spirit. You can open yourself to the help that It's offering you to help you take the next step.

The Golden-tongued Wisdom is Divine Spirit giving us a spiritual message.

*T*he lessons of life are purifying us to make us better beings, to make us better people.

*I*t is very important in this life to learn to love someone more than yourself—whether it's another person or a pet.

We can speak of divine love, but it means nothing unless you've experienced it.

*S*ing HU or some other name of God. It will lift you into the higher levels of spiritual realization.

THE DIVINE KNOWLEDGE

The experiences of life teach truth.

God's love, as it comes down and heals, does things its way.

*T*his is part of the reality of the spiritual path: You're going to meet yourself.

*I*t's better to turn your experiences over to Divine Spirit and just let them come at their natural pace.

We have this knowingness inside that our spiritual life is being taken care of.

What the ECK teachings can do for you is give more insight into life and take away the fear of death.

There's a spiritual bond that connects all Souls: human, animal, and lower forms of life.

*A*nimals are Souls too.

The highest form of love that you can bring into your life is through the Light and Sound of God.

*P*eople with the highest form of love are always serving each other.

*I*n this lifetime we have the opportunity to finally gain the liberty of Soul.

A Giant Hand

A Giant Hand refers to the Holy Spirit helping out in your life and my life in a miraculous way. Sometimes this comes in a quiet way, and sometimes it comes with a loud shout.

*W*hen we first try to be spiritual,
we stumble a lot of the time.

*T*he reason we're here, the reason we are like some gem hidden inside this shell of sand, being ground down, is so that we can become godlike.

This grinding by life works on the pretensions that we have, on our vanity. And gradually we become more of a light— more of a spiritual light—to ourselves and to others.

*

When Divine Spirit does something to help us, it's not simply to cure a symptom.

*W*ho are you? Where have you been? And what does this life mean with all the different experiences that come your way?

*Y*ou are Soul. You are a special being, as is your neighbor.

*W*atch your dreams, and in the morning see if there's a spiritual lesson coming through from the Holy Spirit just for you.

$\mathcal{O}$n the spiritual path, the first step is to love yourself. After this, you grow or develop spiritually so that you can love others who are close to you—your mate, your family. Then you develop the capacity to love people beyond this narrow circle of acquaintance. You grow into a larger circle.

*C*harity is the goodwill we offer to people outside our immediate family and friends. There's a difference between charity—goodwill—and the love we have for our close ones. We have a warm love for those who are close to us. And we certainly should have a warm love for ourselves.

*W*hat's living for? If it's only to put in time—to live to some artificial standard age, to be ready for that last great day—we've wasted our life. If we don't do anything to be there for others when they need us, we've really wasted our lifetime.

*N*early always, when Divine Spirit puts you in an area where someone else is speaking of their heartache, you are there as a vehicle for the Holy Spirit. The Holy Spirit reaches out to that person through you, another human being. Because often the only way people can accept the love and the help of Divine Spirit is through another human being.

So when you make yourself available at times like this—at critical times in other people's lives, at a crossroads—you are being a worker for God, a giant hand.

JUST KEEP MOVING AHEAD

You take life as it comes. You do the best you can. As you learn your lesson, or as you miss your lesson, you move on. You don't look back; you just move on.

The meek shall inherit the earth, but the strong shall inherit heaven.

*P*eople must pay their own debts.
They must reap their own rewards.

*Y*our life will become one of personal responsibility.

*Y*ou become like the duck when the rain falls on it—the rain beads and just rolls off its back. What you've called problems or situations are no longer obstacles holding you back from your own goals in life. You will come to see them as stepping-stones.

*I*f there's one crime—one spiritual crime—that you can do to yourself, it's to not use your God-given creative powers.

When this purifying of Soul begins, Spirit will open up new avenues in our life.

We're so busy just with the survival of our human self that we sometimes forget to be grateful for the very dear things in our lives—our loved ones, our mates and our children, our parents, and our brothers and sisters.

We forget to be grateful for the little things.

*D*reams are important. People around the world study dreams. They realize that this is one of God's ways of speaking to them.

$\mathcal{G}$od can speak to us directly through the Sound or Light. Sometimes in contemplation or during your day you'll see a blue or white light. Know that this is the presence of God. It's the presence of God that's come to uplift you spiritually, to purify your heart, to make you ready for the next step on your journey into the heart of divine love and mercy.

*S*ometimes God speaks through the Sound, and It can be the sound of a musical instrument. It can be one instrument or a number of instruments playing together. It can be the sound of a storm. It can be the sound of thunder. It can be the sound of a drum. It can be the sound of a bird singing. Sometimes It can be the sound of a soft sigh. It can be almost any sound. But if It leaves you uplifted, with a feeling of goodness and love, then you can be assured that this is one of the blessings of God. It was the Voice of God come to uplift you spiritually.

*Y*ou are learning how to get your own answers so that you can go through life with self-mastery.

When you come to the point of self-mastery, you learn that you can shape your own future.

*M*ost people think they are searching for truth when they are really searching for love.

I'd like to wish you well on your journey home and in your quest to find love. Because that is what this journey is all about.

ABOUT THE AUTHOR

Author Harold Klemp is known as a pioneer of today's focus on "everyday spirituality." He was raised on a Wisconsin farm and attended divinity school.

In 1981, after years of training, he became the spiritual leader of Eckankar, Religion of the Light and Sound of God. His mission is to help people find their way back to God in this life.

Harold Klemp speaks each year to thousands of seekers at Eckankar seminars. Author of more than forty-five books, he continues to write, including many articles and spiritual-study discourses. Harold Klemp's inspiring and practical approach to spirituality helps thousands of people worldwide find greater freedom, wisdom, and love in their lives.

ALSO BY
HAROLD KLEMP

Available at bookstores, online booksellers,
or directly from:
Eckankar
P.O. Box 27300 Minneapolis, MN 55427
Tel (952) 380-2200 Fax (952) 380-2295
www.eckankar.org

Immortality of Soul Series
The Language of Soul
Love—The Keystone of Life

A selected list:
Autobiography of a Modern Prophet
A Modern Prophet Answers Your Key Questions about Life